Caruso and Tetrazzini
on
THE ART
OF SINGING

Caruso and Tetrazzini
on
THE ART
OF SINGING

By Enrico Caruso
and Luisa Tetrazzini

Dover Publications, Inc., New York

Published in Canada by General Publishing Company, Ltd., 30 Lesmill Road, Don Mills, Toronto, Ontario.
Published in the United Kingdom by Constable and Company, Ltd.

This Dover edition, first published in 1975, is an unabridged and unaltered republication of the work originally published by The Metropolitan Company, Publishers, New York, in 1909.

International Standard Book Number: 0-486-23140-2
Library of Congress Catalog Card Number: 74-84048

Manufactured in the United States of America
Dover Publications, Inc.
180 Varick Street
New York, N.Y. 10014

PREFACE

IN OFFERING this work to the public the publishers wish to lay before those who sing or who are about to study singing, the simple, fundamental rules of the art based on common sense. The two greatest living exponents of the art of singing—Luisa Tetrazzini and Enrico Caruso—have been chosen as examples, and their talks on singing have additional weight from the fact that what they have to say has been printed exactly as it was uttered, the truths they expound are driven home forcefully, and what they relate so simply is backed by years of experience and emphasized by the results they have achieved as the two greatest artists in the world.

Much has been said about the Italian Method of Singing. It is a question whether anyone really knows what the phrase means. After all, if there be a right way to sing, then all other ways must be wrong. Books have been written on breathing, tone production and what singers should eat and wear, etc., etc., all tending to make the singer self-conscious and to sing with the brain rather than with the heart. To quote Mme. Tetrazzini: "You can train the voice, you can take a raw material and make it a finished production; not so with the heart."

The country is overrun with inferior teachers of singing; men and women who have failed to get before the

public, turn to teaching without any practical experience, and, armed only with a few methods, teach these
alike to all pupils, ruining many good voices. Should
these pupils change teachers, even for the better, then
begins the weary undoing of the false method, often
with no better result.

To these unfortunate pupils this book is of inestimable
value. He or she could not consistently choose such
teachers after reading its pages. Again the simple
rules laid down and tersely and interestingly set forth
not only carry conviction with them, but tear away the
veil of mystery that so often is thrown about the divine
art.

Luisa Tetrazzini and Enrico Caruso show what not
to do, as well as what to do, and bring the pupil back
to first principles—the art of singing naturally.

THE ART
OF SINGING

By Luisa Tetrazzini

LUISA TETRAZZINI

LUISA TETRAZZINI

L UISA TETRAZZINI, the most famous Italian
coloratura soprano of the day, declares that she
began to sing before she learned to talk. Her
parents were not musical, but her elder sister, now
the wife of the eminent conductor Cleofante Campanini, was a public singer of established reputation,
and her success roused her young sister's ambition to
become a great artist. Her parents were well to do,
her father having a large army furnishing store in
Florence, and they did not encourage her in her determination to become a prima donna. One prima donna,
said her father, was enough for any family.

Luisa did not agree with him. If one prima donna is
good, she argued, why would not two be better? So
she never desisted from her importunity until she was
permitted to become a pupil of Professor Coccherani,
vocal instructor at the Lycée. At this time she had
committed to memory more than a dozen grand opera
rôles, and at the end of six months the professor con-
fessed that he could do nothing more for her voice; that
she was ready for a career.

She made her bow to the Florentine opera going
public, one of the most critical in Italy, as Inez, in
Meyerbeer's "L'Africaine," and her success was so
pronounced that she was engaged at a salary of $100 a
month, a phenomenal beginning for a young singer.
Queen Margherita was present on the occasion and com-

plimented her highly and prophesied for her a great career. She asked the trembling débutante how old she was, and in the embarrassment of the moment Luisa made herself six years older than she really was. This is one noteworthy instance in which a public singer failed to discount her age.

Fame came speedily, but for a long time it was confined to Europe and Latin America. She sang seven seasons in St. Petersburg, three in Mexico, two in Madrid, four in Buenos Aires, and even on the Pacific coast of America before she appeared in New York. She had sung Lucia more than 200 times before her first appearance at Covent Garden, and the twenty curtain calls she received on that occasion came as the greatest surprise of her career. She had begun to believe that she could never be appreciated by English-speaking audiences and the ovation almost overcame her.

It was by the merest chance that Mme. Tetrazzini ever came to the Manhattan Opera House in New York. The diva's own account of her engagement is as follows:

"I was in London, and for a wonder I had a week, a wet week, on my hands. You know people will do anything in a wet week in London.

"There were contracts from all over the Continent and South America pending. There was much discussion naturally in regard to settlements and arrangements of one kind and another.

"Suddenly, just like that"—she makes a butterfly gesture—"M. Hammerstein came, and just like that"—a duplicate gesture—"I made up my mind that I would come here. If his offer to me had been seven days later I should not have signed, and if I had not I should undoubtedly never have come, for a contract that I might have signed to go elsewhere would probably have been for a number of years."

Voice experts confess that they are not able to solve the mystery of Mme. Tetrazzini's wonderful management of her breathing.

"It is perfectly natural," she says. "I breathe low down in the diaphragm, not, as some do, high up in the upper part of the chest. I always hold some breath in reserve for the crescendos, employing only what is absolutely necessary, and I renew the breath wherever it is easiest.

"In breathing I find, as in other matters pertaining to singing, that as one goes on and practices, no matter how long one may have been singing, there are constantly new surprises awaiting one. You may have been accustomed for years to take a note in a certain way, and after a long while you discover that, while it is a very good way, there is a better."

```
*******************************************************
*                                                     *
*              Breath Control                         *
*         The Foundation of Singing                   *
*                                                     *
*******************************************************
```

THERE is only one way to sing correctly, and that is to sing naturally, easily, comfortably.

The height of vocal art is to have no apparent method, but to be able to sing with perfect facility from one end of the voice to the other, emitting all the notes clearly and yet with power and having each note of the scale sound the same in quality and tonal beauty as the ones before and after.

There are many methods which lead to the goal of natural singing—that is to say, the production of the voice with ease, beauty and with perfect control.

Some of the greatest teachers in the world reach this point apparently by diverging roads.

Around the art of singing there has been formed a cult which includes an entire jargon of words meaning one thing to the singer and another thing to the rest of the world and which very often doesn't mean the same thing to two singers of different schools.

In these talks with you I am going to try to use the simplest words, and the few idioms which I will have to take from my own language I will translate to you as clearly as I can, so that there can be no misunderstanding.

Certainly the highest art and a lifetime of work and study are necessary to acquire an easy emission of tone.

There are quantities of wonderful natural voices, particularly among the young people of Switzerland and Italy, and the American voice is especially noted for its purity and the beauty of its tone in the high registers.

But these naturally untrained voices soon break or fail if they are used much unless the singer supplements the natural, God-given vocal gifts with a conscious understanding of how the vocal apparatus should be used.

The singer must have some knowledge of his or her anatomical structure, particularly the structure of the throat, mouth and face, with its resonant cavities, which are so necessary for the right production of the voice.

Besides that, the lungs and diaphragm and the whole breathing apparatus must be understood, because the foundation of singing is breathing and breath control.

A singer must be able to rely on his breath, just as he relies upon the solidity of the ground beneath his feet.

A shaky, uncontrolled breath is like a rickety foundation on which nothing can be built, and until that foundation has been developed and strengthened the would-be singer need expect no satisfactory results.

From the girls to whom I am talking especially I must now ask a sacrifice—the singer cannot wear tight corsets and should not wear corsets of any kind which come up higher than the lowest rib.

In other words, the corset must be nothing but a belt, but with as much hip length as the wearer finds convenient and necessary.

In order to insure proper breathing capacity it is understood that the clothing must be absolutely loose around the chest and also across the lower part of the back, for one should breathe with the back of the lungs as well as with the front.

In my years of study and work I have developed my own breathing capacity until I am somewhat the despair of the fashionable modiste, but I have a diaphragm and a breath on which I can rely at all times.

In learning to breathe it is well to think of the lungs

as empty sacks, into which the air is dropping like a weight, so that you think first of filling the bottom of your lungs, then the middle part, and so on until no more air can be inhaled.

Inhale short breaths through the nose. This, of course, is only an exercise for breath development.

Now begin to inhale from the bottom of the lungs first.

Exhale slowly and feel as if you were pushing the air against your chest. If you can get this sensation later when singing it will help you very greatly to get control of the breath and to avoid sending too much breath through the vocal chords.

The breath must be sent out in an even, steady flow.

You will notice when you begin to sing, if you watch yourself very carefully, that, first, you will try to inhale too much air; secondly, you will either force it all out at once, making a breathy note, or in trying to control the flow of air by the diaphragm you will suddenly cease to send it forth at all and will be making the sound by pressure from the throat.

There must never be any pressure from the throat. The sound must be made from the continued flow of air.

You must learn to control this flow of air, so that no muscular action of the throat can shut it off.

Open the throat wide and start your note by the pressure breath. The physical sensation should be first an effort on the part of the diaphragm to press the air up against the chest box, then the sensation of a perfectly open throat, and, lastly, the sensation that the air is passing freely into the cavities of the head.

The quantity of sound is controlled by the breath.

In diminishing the tone the opening of the throat remains the same. Only the quantity of breath given forth is diminished. That is done by the diaphragm muscles.

"Filare la voce," to spin the voice from a tiny little thread into a breadth of sound and then diminish again, is one of the most beautiful effects in singing.

It is accomplished by the control of the breath, and its perfect accomplishment means the complete mastery of the greatest difficulty in learning to sing.

I think one of the best exercises for learning to control the voice by first getting control of the breath is to stand erect in a well-ventilated room or out of doors and slowly snuff in air through the nostrils, inhaling in little puffs, as if you were smelling something.

Take just a little bit of air at a time and feel as if you were filling the very bottom of your lungs and also the back of your lungs.

When you have the sensation of being full up to the neck retain the air for a few seconds and then very slowly send it out in little puffs again.

This is a splendid exercise, but I want to warn you not to practise any breathing exercise to such an extent that you make your heart beat fast or feel like strangling.

Overexercising the lungs is as bad as not exercising them enough and the results are often harmful.

Like everything else in singing, you want to learn this gradually. Never neglect it, because it is the very foundation of your art. But don't try to develop a diaphragm expansion of five inches in two weeks.

Indeed, it is not the expansion that you are working for.

I have noticed this one peculiarity about young singers—if they have an enormous development of the diaphragm they think they should be able to sing, no matter what happens. A girl came to see me once whose figure was really entirely out of proportion, the lower part of the lungs having been pressed out quite beyond even artistic lines.

"You see, madam," she exclaimed, "I have studied breathing. Why, I have such a strong diaphragm I can move the piano with it!" And she did go right up to my piano and, pushing on this strong diaphragm of hers, moved the piano a fraction of an inch from its place.

I was quite aghast. I had never met such an athletic singer. When I asked her to let me hear her voice, however, a tiny stream of contralto sound issued from those powerful lungs.

She had developed her breathing capacity, but when she sang she held her breath back.

I have noticed that a great many people do this, and it is one of the things that must be overcome in the very beginning of the study of singing.

Certain young singers take in an enormous breath, stiffening every muscle in order to hold the air, thus depriving their muscles of all elasticity.

They will then shut off the throat and let only the smallest fraction of air escape, just enough to make a sound. Too much inbreathing and too violent an effort at inhaling will not help the singer at all.

People have said that they cannot see when I breathe. Well, they certainly cannot say that I am ever short of breath even if I do try to breathe invisibly. When I breathe I scarcely draw my diaphragm in at all, but I feel the air fill my lungs and I feel my upper ribs expand.

In singing I always feel as if I were forcing my breath against my chest, and, just as in the exercises according to Delsarte you will find the chest leads in all physical movements, so in singing you should feel this firm support of the chest of the highest as well as the lowest notes.

I have seen pupils, trying to master the art of breathing, holding themselves as rigidly as drum majors.

Now this rigidity of the spinal column will in no way help you in the emission of tone, nor will it increase the breath control. In fact, I don't think it would even help you to stand up straight, although it would certainly give one a stiff appearance and one far removed from grace.

A singer should stand freely and easily and should feel as if the chest were leading, but should not feel constrained or stiff in any part of the ribs or lungs.

From the minute the singer starts to emit a tone the supply of breath must be emitted steadily from the chamber of air in the lungs. It must never be held back once.

The immediate pressure of the air should be felt more against the chest. I know of a great many singers who, when they come to very difficult passages, put their hands on their chests, focusing their attention on this one part of the mechanism of singing.

The audience, of course, thinks the prima donna's hand is raised to her heart, when, as a matter of fact, the prima donna, with a difficult bit of singing before her, is thinking of her technique and the foundation of that technique—breath control.

This feeling of singing against the chest with the weight of air pressing up against it is known as "breath support," and in Italian we have even a better word, "apoggio," which is breath prop. The diaphragm in

English may be called the bellows of the lungs, but the apoggio is the deep breath regulated by the diaphragm.

The attack of the sound must come from the apoggio, or breath prop. In attacking the very highest notes it is essential, and no singer can really get the high notes or vocal flexibility or strength of tone without the attack coming from this seat of respiration.

In practising the trill or staccato tones the pressure of the breath must be felt even before the sound is heard. The beautiful, clear, bell-like tones that die away into a soft piano are tones struck on the apoggio and controlled by the steady soft pressure of the breath emitted through a perfectly open throat, over a low tongue and resounding in the cavities of the mouth or head.

Never for a moment sing without this apoggio, this breath prop. Its development and its constant use mean the restoration of sick or fatigued voices and the prolonging of all one's vocal powers into what is wrongly called old age.

The Mastery of the Tongue

THE tongue is a veritable stumbling block in the path of the singer. The tongue is an enormous muscle compared with the other parts of the throat and mouth, and its roots particularly can by a slight movement block the passage of the throat pressing against the larynx. This accounts for much of the pinched singing we hear.

When the tongue forms a mountain in the back part of the mouth the singer produces what you call in English slang "a hot potato tone"—that is to say, a tone that sounds as if it were having much difficulty to get through the mouth. In very fact, it is having this difficulty, for it has to pass over the back of the tongue.

The would-be singer has to learn to control the tongue muscles and, above all things, to learn to relax the tongue and to govern it at will, so that it never stiffens and forms that hard lump which can be plainly felt immediately beneath the chin under the jaw.

It requires a great deal of practice to gain control of the tongue, and there are many different exercises which purport to be beneficial in gaining complete mastery over it. One, for instance, is to throw the tongue out as far forward as possible without stiffening it and then draw it back slowly. This can be done in front of a mirror by trying to throw the tongue not only from the tip, but from the root, keeping the sides of the tongue broad. Another way is to catch hold of the two sides of the tongue with the fingers and pull it out gently.

17

For my part, I scarcely approve of these mechanical ways of gaining control of the tongue except in cases where the singer is phlegmatic of temperament and cannot be made to feel the various sensations of stiff tongue or tongue drawn far back in other ways. Ordinarily I think they make the singer conscious, nervous and more likely to stiffen the tongue in a wild desire to relax it and keep it flat.

These exercises, however, combined with exercises in diction, help to make the tongue elastic, and the more elastic and quick this muscle becomes the clearer will be the singer's diction and the more flexible will be her voice.

The correct position of the tongue is raised from the back, lying flat in the mouth, the flattened tip beneath the front teeth, with the sides slightly raised so as to form a slight furrow in it. When the tongue is lying too low a lump under the chin beneath the jaw will form in singing and the tight muscles can be easily felt.

When the jaw is perfectly relaxed and the tongue lies flat in the mouth there will be a slight hollow under the chin and no stiffness in the muscles.

The tip of the tongue of course is employed in the pronunciation of the consonants and must be so agile that the minute it has finished its work it at once resumes the correct position.

In ascending the scale the furrow in the tongue increases as we come to the higher notes. It is here that the back of the palate begins to draw up in order to add to the resonance of the head notes, giving the cavities of the head free play.

You can easily see your back palate working by opening your mouth wide and giving yourself the sensation of one about to sneeze. You will see far back in the throat, way behind the nose, a soft spot that will draw up of itself as the sneeze becomes more imminent. That little point is the soft palate. It must be drawn up for the high notes in order to get the head resonance. As a singer advances in her art she can do this at will.

The adjustment of throat, tongue and palate, all working together, will daily respond more easily to her demands. However, she should be able consciously to control each part by itself.

The conscious direction of the voice and command of the throat are necessary. Frequently in opera the singer, sitting or lying in some uncomfortable position which is not naturally convenient for producing the voice, will consciously direct her notes into the head cavities by opening up the throat and lifting the soft palate. For instance, in the role of Violetta the music of the last act is sung lying down. In order to get proper resonance to some of the high notes I have to start them in the head cavity by means, of course, of the apoggio, or breath prop, without which the note would be thin and would have no body to it.

The sensation that I have is of a slight pressure of breath striking almost into a direct line into the cavity behind the forehead over the eyes without any obstruction or feeling in the throat at all.

This is the correct attack for the head tone, or a tone taken in the upper register. Before I explain the registers to you I must tell you one of the funniest compliments I ever received. A very flattering person was comparing my voice to that of another high soprano whom I very much admire.

"Her voice is beautiful, particularly in the upper register," I insisted when the other lady was being criticized.

"Ah, madame," responded the flattering critic, "but your registers give out so much more warmth."

I think this joke is too good to lose, also the criticism, while unjust to the other singer, is interesting to the student, because in the high register, which includes in some voices all the notes above middle C, the notes are thin and cold unless supported by the apoggio, the breath prop, of which I have told you so much. People ask whether there are such things as vocal registers. Certainly there are. There are three always and sometimes four in very high voices. The ordinary registers are the low, the middle, the high voice, or head voice, and sometimes the second high voice, which has been called the flagellant voice.

A vocal register is a series of tones which are produced by a certain position of the larynx, tongue and palate. In the woman's voice the middle register takes in the notes from E on the first line of the staff about to middle C. The head voice begins at middle C and runs up sometimes to the end of the voice, sometimes to B flat or C, where it joins the second head register, which I have heard ascend into a whistle in phenomenal voices cultivated only in this register and useless for vocal work.

Though the registers exist and the tones in middle, below and above are not produced in the same manner, the voice should be so equalized that the change in registers cannot be heard. And a tone sung with a head voice and in the low voice should have the same degree of quality, resonance and power.

As the voice ascends in the scale each note is different, and as one goes on up the positions of the organ of the throat cannot remain the same for several different tones. But there should never be an abrupt change, either audible to the audience or felt in the singer's throat. Every tone must be imperceptibly prepared, and upon the elasticity of the vocal organs depends the smoothness of the tone production. Adjusting the vocal apparatus to the high register should be both imperceptible and mechanical whenever a high note has to be sung.

In the high register the head voice, or voice which vibrates in the head cavities, should be used chiefly. The middle register requires palatal resonance, and the first notes of the head register and the last ones of the middle require a judicious blending of both. The middle register can be dragged up to the high notes, but always at the cost first of the beauty of the voice and then of the voice itself, for no organ can stand being used wrongly for a long time.

This is only one of the reasons that so many fine big voices go to pieces long before they should.

In an excess of enthusiasm the young singer attempts to develop the high notes and make them sound—in her own ears, at all events—as big as the middle voice. The pure head tone sounds small and feeble to the singer herself, and she would rather use the chest quality, but the head tone has the piercing, penetrating quality which makes it tell in a big hall, while the middle register, unless used in its right place, makes the voice muffled, heavy and lacking in vibrancy. Though to the singer the tone may seem immense, in reality it lacks resonance.

A singer must never cease listening to herself intelligently and never neglect cultivating the head tone or over-tone of the voice, which is its salvation, for it means vibrancy, carrying power and youth to a voice. Without it the finest voice soon becomes worn and off pitch. Used judiciously it will preserve a voice into old age.

```
********************************************
*                                          *
*         Tone  Emission  and  Attack      *
*                                          *
********************************************
```

Tone Emission and Attack

IN my first talk I said a few words, but not half
enough, on the subject of breath control.
My second talk was the physiological aspect of
the throat, head and tongue, for it is necessary to
become thoroughly acquainted with the mechanism
with which you are to work before you can really sing.
Today I'm going to take up the subject of tone emission
and the attack.

A great many singers suffer from the defect called
"throatiness" of the emission—that is to say, they
attack or start the note in the throat.   Sooner or later
this attack will ruin the most beautiful voice.   As I
have said before, the attack of the note must come
from the apoggio, or breath prop.   But to have the
attack pure and perfectly in tune you must have the
throat entirely open, for it is useless to try to sing if the
throat is not sufficiently open to let the sound pass
freely.   Throaty tones or pinched tones are tones which
are trying to force themselves through a half-closed
throat blocked either by insufficient opening of the
larynx or by stoppage of the throat passage, due to the
root of the tongue being forced down and back too hard
or possibly to a low, soft palate.

In order to have the throat perfectly open it is necessary to have the jaw absolutely relaxed.

I have found in studying different nationalities
that it is fairly easy for the French and Spanish people
to learn this relaxation of jaw and the opening of the
throat, but the English-speaking people generally talk
with the throat half shut and even talk through half-

shut teeth. Sometime, when you are talking rapidly, suddenly put your hand up to your jaw. You will find that it is stiff; that the muscles beneath it (tongue muscles) are tight and hard; that the jaw seldom goes down very far in pronouncing any of the English words, whereas in singing the jaw should be absolutely relaxed, going down and back just as far as it can with ease.

The jaw is attached to the skull right beneath the temples in front of the ears. By placing your two fingers there and dropping the jaw you will find that a space between the skull and jaw grows as the jaw drops.

In singing this space must be as wide as is possible, for that indicates that the jaw is dropped down, giving its aid to the opening at the back of the throat. It will help the beginner sometimes to do simple relaxing exercises, feeling the jaw drop with the fingers. It must drop down, and it is not necessary to open the mouth wide, because the jaw is relaxed to its utmost.

However, for a beginner it is as well to practice opening the mouth wide, being sure to lower the jaw at the back. Do this many times a day without emitting any sound merely to get the feeling of what an open throat is really like. You will presently begin to yawn after you have done the exercise a couple of times. In yawning or in starting to drink a sip of water the throat is widely open, and the sensation is a correct one which the singer must study to reproduce.

I have noticed a great many actors and actresses in America who speak with jaws tightly closed, or at least closed to such an extent that only the smallest emission of breath is possible. Such a voice production will never allow the actor to express any varying degree of emotion and will also completely eradicate any natural beauty of tone which the voice may have. However,

this is a fault which can easily be overcome by practicing
this daily relaxation of the jaw and always when singing
breathing as if the jaw hung perfectly loose, or, better
still, as if you had none at all. When you can see a vocalist pushing on the jaw you can be perfectly certain
that the tone she is emitting at that moment is a forced
note and that the whole vocal apparatus is being tor-
tured to create what is probably not a pleasant noise.

Any kind of mental distress will cause the jaw to
stiffen and will have an immediate effect upon the
voice. This is one of the reasons why a singer must
learn to control her emotions and must not subject
herself to any harrowing experiences, even such as
watching a sensational spectacle, before she is going to
sing. Fear, worry, fright—stage as well as other
kinds—set the jaw. So does too great a determination
to succeed. A singer's mind must control all of her
feelings if it is going to control her voice. She must
be able even to surmount a feeling of illness or stage
fright and to control her vocal apparatus, as well as her
breath, no matter what happens.

The singer should feel as if her jaw were detached and
falling away from her face. As one great singer ex-
presses it: "You should have the jaw of an imbecile
when emitting a tone. In fact, you shouldn't know
that you have one."   Let us take the following passage
from "The Marriage of Figaro," by Mozart:

Voi-che sa-pe-te-

This would make an excellent exercise for the jaw.
Sing only the vowels, dropping the jaw as each one is
attacked—"o, eh, ah."   The o, of course, is pronounced

like the English o and the i in voi like e.   The e in che is pronounced like the English a.   Sapete is pronounced sahpata.   You now have the vowels, o, ee, a, ah, a. Open the throat wide, drop the jaw and pronounce the tones on a note in the easiest part of your voice.

Do not attack a note at the same time that you are inhaling.   That is too soon.   Take the breath through the nose, of course, and give it an instant to settle before attacking the sound.   In this way you will avoid the stroke of the glottis which is caused by the sudden and uncontrolled emission of the accumulated breath.   In attacking a note the breath must be directed to the focusing point on the palate which lies just at the critical spot, different for every tone.   In attacking a note, however, there must be no pressure on this place, because if there is the overtones will be unable to soar and sound with the tone.

From the moment the note is attacked the breath must flow out with it.   It is a good idea to feel at first as if one were puffing out the breath.   This is particularly good for the high notes on which a special stress must be laid always to attack with the breath and not to press or push with the throat.   As long as the tone lasts the gentle but uninterrupted outpouring of the breath must continue behind it.   This breath pressure insures the strength and, while holding the note to the focusing point on the palate, insures its pitch.   In a general way it can be said that the medium tones of the voice have their focusing point in the middle part of the palate, the lower tones coming nearer to the teeth to be centralized and the high notes giving the sensation of finding their focusing point in the high arch at the back of the mouth and going out, as it were, through the crown of the head.

The resonance in the head cavities is soon perceived by those who are beginning to sing. Sometimes in producing their first high notes young people become nervous and irritated when singing high tones at the curious buzzing in the head and ears. After a short time, however, this sensation is no longer an irritation, and the singer can gauge in a way where his tones are placed by getting a mental idea of where the resonance to each particular tone should be.

High notes with plenty of head vibration can only be obtained when the head is clear and the nasal cavities unobstructed by mucous membrane or by any of the depression which comes from physical or mental cause. The best way to lose such depression is to practice. Practicing the long scale, being careful to use the different registers, as described later, will almost invariably even out the voice and clear out the head if continued long enough, and will enable the singer to overcome nervous or mental depression as well.

The different sensations in producing the tone vary according to the comparative height and depth. Beginning from the medium tones, the singer will feel as if each tone of the descending scale were being sung farther outside of the mouth, the vibration hitting the upper teeth as it goes out, whereas with the ascending scale the vibrations pass through the nasal cavities, through the cavity in the forehead and up back into the head, until one feels as if the tone were being formed high over the head at the back.

I want to say right here that whenever a young singer feels uncomfortable when singing he or she is singing incorrectly.

In attacking the note on the breath, particularly in the high notes, it is quite possible that at first the voice

will not respond. For a long time merely an emission
or breath or perhaps a little squeak on the high note is
all that can be hoped for. If, however, this is continued, eventually the head voice will be joined to the
breath, and a faint note will find utterance which with
practice will develop until it becomes an easy and
brilliant tone.

The reason that the tone has not been able to come
forth is because the vocal apparatus cannot adjust itself
to the needs of the vocal chords or because they themselves have not accustomed themselves to respond to
the will of the singer and are too stiff to perform their
duty.

The scale is the greatest test of voice production.
No opera singer, no concert singer, who cannot sing a
perfect scale can be said to be a technician or to have
achieved results in her art. Whether the voice be soprano, mezzo or contralto, each note should be perfect
of its kind, and the note of each register should partake
sufficiently of the quality of the next register above or
below it in order not to make the transition noticeable
when the voice ascends or descends the scale. This
blending of the registers is obtained by the intelligence
of the singer in mixing the different tone qualities of
the registers, using as aids the various formations of the
lips, mouth and throat and the ever present apoggio
without which no perfect scale can be sung.

Facial Expression and Mirror Practice

IN studying a new rôle I am in the habit of practicing in front of a mirror in order to get an idea of the effect of a facial expression and to see that it does not take away from the correct position of the mouth.

The young singer should practice constantly in front of a mirror as soon as she begins to sing songs or to express emotions in her music, for the girl with the expressive face is likely to contort her mouth so that the correct emission of tones is impossible.

The dramatic artist depends largely for her expression on the changing lines of the mouth, chin and jaw, and in any lines spoken which denote command or will you will see the actor's jaw setting and becoming rigid with the rest of the facial mask.

Now, a singer can never allow the facial expression to alter the position of the jaw or mouth. Facial expression for the singer must concern itself chiefly with the eyes and forehead.

The mouth must remain the same, and the jaw must ever be relaxed, whether the song is one of deep intensity or a merry scale of laughter.

The mouth in singing should always smile lightly. This slight smile at once relaxes the lips, allowing them free play for the words which they and the tongue must form and also gives the singer a slight sensation of uplift necessary for singing.

It is impossible to sing well when mentally depressed or even physically indisposed slightly. Unless one has complete control over the entire vocal apparatus and unless one can simulate a smile one does not feel the voice will lack some of its resonant quality, particularly in the upper notes, where the smiling position of the mouth adjusts the throat and air passages for the emission of light tones.

The lips are of the greatest aid in shaping and shading the tones. Wagnerian singers, for instance, who employ trumpet-like notes in certain passages are often seen shaping their lips like the mouthpiece of a trumpet, with a somewhat square opening, the lips protruding.

However, this can be practiced only after perfect relaxation of the jaw and control of the tongue have been accomplished.

A singer's mouth must always look pleasant, not only because it creates a disagreeable impression on the audience to see a crooked and contorted mouth, but also because natural and correct voice production requires a mouth shaped almost into a smile.

Too wide a smile often accompanies what is called "the white voice." This is a voice production where a head resonance alone is employed, without sufficient of the apoggio or enough of the mouth resonance to give the tone a vital quality. This "white voice" should be thoroughly understood and is one of the many shades of tone a singer can use at times, just as the impressionist uses various unusual colors to produce certain atmospheric effects.

For instance, in the mad scene in "Lucia" the use of the "white voice" suggests the babbling of the mad woman, as the same voice in the last act of "Traviata" or in the last act of "Bohemè" suggests utter physical exhaustion and the approach of death.

An entire voice production on these colorless lines, however, would always lack the brilliancy and the vitality which inspire enthusiasm.

One of the compensations of the "white voice" singer is the fact that she usually possesses a perfect diction. The voice itself is thrust into the head cavities and not allowed to vibrate in the face and mouth and gives ample room for the formation of vowels and consonants. And the singer with this voice production usually concentrates her entire attention on diction.

The cure for this tone emission is, first of all, the cultivation of the breath prop, then attacking the vowel sound o o in the medium voice, which requires a low position of the larynx, and exercises on the ascending scale until the higher notes have been brought down, as it were, and gain some of the body and support of the lower notes without losing their quality.

The singer's expression must concern itself chiefly with the play of emotion around the eyes, eyebrows and forehead. You have no idea how much expression you can get out of your eyebrows, for instance, until you study the question and learn by experiment that a complete emotional scale can be symbolized outwardly in the movements of the eyelids and eyebrows.

A very drooping eyebrow is expressive of fatigue, either physical or mental. This lowered eyelid is the aspect we see about us most of the time, particularly on people past their first youth. As it shows a lack of interest, it is not a favorite expression of actors and is only employed where the rôle makes it necessary.

Increasing anxiety is depicted by slanting the eyebrows obliquely in a downward line toward the nose.

Concentrated attention draws the eyebrows together over the bridge of the nose, while furtiveness widens the space again without elevating the eyebrows.

In the eyebrows alone you can depict mockery, every

stage of anxiety or pain, astonishment, ecstasy, terror, suffering, fury and admiration, besides all the subtle tones between.

In singing rôles of songs it is necessary to practice before the mirror in order to see that this facial expression is present and that it is not exaggerated; that the face is not contorted by lines of suffering or by the lines of mirth.

Another thing the young singer must not forget in making her initial bow before the public is the question of dress. When singing on the platform or stage, dress as well as you can. Whenever you face the public have at least the assurance you are looking your very best; that your gowns hang well, are well fitted and are of a becoming color.

It is not necessary that they should be gorgeous or expensive, but let them always be suitable, and for big cities let them be just as sumptuous as you can afford. At morning concerts in New York, velvets and hand-painted chiffons are considered good form, while in the afternoon handsome silk or satin frocks of a very light color are worn with hats.

If a singer chooses to wear a hat let her be sure that its shape will not interfere with her voice.

A very large hat, for instance, with a wide brim that comes down over the face, acts as a sort of blanket to the voice, eating up the sound and detracting from the beauty of tone, which should go forth into the audience. It is also likely to shade the singer's features too much and hide her from view from those sitting in the balconies or galleries. As a rule, the singer's hat should be small or with a flaring brim, which does not detract from the tone.

Another word on the subject of corsets. There is

no reason in the world why a singer should not wear corsets, and if singers have a tendency to grow stout a corset is usually a necessity. A singer's corset should be especially well fitted around the hips and should be extremely loose over the diaphragm.

If made in this way it will not interfere in the slightest degree with the breath.

Now as to diet and the general mode of life. Every singer must take care of her health. But that does not necessarily mean that she must wrap herself in cotton batting and lead a sequestered existence. I don't believe that any person who wants to make a public career can accomplish it and also indulge in social dissipations. Society must be cut out of the life of the would-be singer, for the demands made by it on time and vitality can only be given at a sacrifice to one's art.

The care of the health is an individual matter, and what agrees well with me would cause others to sicken. I eat the simplest food always, and naturally, being an Italian, I prefer the food of my native land. But simple French or German cookery agrees with me quite as well. And I allow the tempting pastry, the rich and overspiced pâté, to pass me by untouched and console myself with quantities of fruit and fresh vegetables.

Personally I never wear a collar and have hardened my throat to a considerable extent by wearing slightly cutout gowns always in the house, and even when I wear furs I do not have them closely drawn around the neck. I try to keep myself at an even bodily temperature, and fresh air has been my most potent remedy at all times when I have been indisposed.

Appreciative Attitude and Critical Attitude

THERE is nothing so beneficial to the young artist as the kindly and just criticism of a person who knows and nothing so stimulating as his praise.

Among my most priceless possessions I treasure the words of encouragement given me by Patti and Sembrich, those wonderful artists, when I was beginning my career.

Mme. Patti is a splendid example of the many sidedness necessary to artistic perfection. Her wonderful voice was always supplemented by complete knowledge of the art of singing, and her mastery of languages and of different fields of art made her not only a great artist, but a most interesting woman.

To hear an artist of this kind is one of the most profitable parts of a musical education.

But there are two ways of listening to a singer. There is the appreciative way, and there is the entirely critical. The beginner usually tries to show her knowledge by her intensely critical attitude.

The older you become in your art the more readily you will be able to appreciate and learn from the singers you hear on the opera or concert stage.

The greatest and the humblest singer can teach you something. But to learn you must be in a receptive attitude.

The public has no real conception of what an amount of intelligent work besides talent and art is necessary to achieve the results which it sees or hears. Only those whose lives are devoted to the same ideals can understand the struggles of other artists, and it is for that reason that appreciation and not condemnation should be on the tongues of those who themselves have studied.

The artist may demand the greatest things of herself, and what may be good enough for others is not good enough for her. As the poet says, "Art is long," though life may be short, and singing is one of the most fleeting of all arts, since once the note is uttered it leaves only a memory in the hearer's mind and since so many beautiful voices, for one reason or other, go to pieces long before their time.

If the singer's health is good the voice should end only with life itself, provided, of course, it has been used with understanding and with art.

In performing before the public one should be governed by the tastes of the public, not by one's own tastes. Just as the comedian usually wishes to play Hamlet and the man of tragic mien thinks he could be a comedy star, the singer who could make a fortune at interpreting chansonnettes usually wishes to sing operatic roles, and the singer with a deep and heavy voice is longing to inflict baby songs on a long suffering public.

It is easy enough to find out what the public wishes to hear, and, though one should always be enlarging one's repertory, it is not a bad idea to stick to that field for which one is particularly fitted vocally and physically.

In studying a rôle after one has mastered the technical difficulties one should try to steep one's personality into that of the character one is to portray, and for that reason all study, no matter what it is, and reading of all kinds help one in developing a part.

The great Italian tragedienne, Duse, told me that
one of her greatest pleasures was to wander about the
streets incognito watching the types of people, following them round, observing them in their daily lives
and remembering all the small details of action,
gesture or expression which she could some day
embody into a rôle.

The more one sees and studies people with sympathy,
the more points one gets for the study of life which is
embodied in the art one gives forth. But it is sympathy
with one's fellow beings and kindly observation
which help one here, never the critical attitude.

An artist can only afford to be coldly critical toward
his own work and not toward the work of others.

Recently a young woman who started her vocal
career as a contralto has sung the most difficult of
Wagnerian soprano parts. Her high notes, it is true,
were not the high notes of a natural soprano voice,
but the care and perfection with which each high
note was attacked were worthy of closest attention
and admiration and defied criticism.

Hearing the smaller singers, the beginners who
are still struggling with their art, should awaken in
the heart of the intelligent listener not contemptuous
criticism, but should be one means of realizing one's
own vocal defects and the possible ways of overcoming
them.

There are bad singing teachers, of course, but often
the pupils are worse and will not listen to advice. The
large and shrieking voice usually belongs to this type
of pupil, for it is easier to force the voice when the
temperament is robust and the vocal cords equally
strong than it is to learn gently and quietly the correct
and natural position in voice placement, and it is

easier to make a noise as best you can than to use intelligently the different resonance cavities for the blending of the perfect tone.

Another fault severely criticised in the youthful singer is a lack of correct pronunciation or diction. It is only after the voice is perfectly controlled that the lips and tongue can function freely for the pronunciation of syllables.

While the voice is in what might be called a state of ferment the singer is only anxious to produce tones, and diction slips by the wayside. The appreciative listener should be able to know whether a lack of diction on the singer's part means immaturity or simply slovenliness.

Still another fault in voice production is the tremolo. It is the overambitious singer, the singer who forces a small, light organ to do heavy work, who develops the tremolo.

The tremolo is a sure sign that the vocal chords have been stretched beyond their natural limits, and there is only one thing can cure this. That is absolute rest for some time and then beginning the study of the voice, first singing with the mouth closed and relying entirely on very gentle breath pressure for the production of the sound.

The pupil suffering from tremolo or even very strong vibrato must have courage to stop at once and to forego having a big voice. After all, the most beautiful voices in the world are not necessarily the biggest voices, and certainly the tremolo is about the worst fault a singer can have. But that, like almost any other vocal defect, can be cured by persistent effort of the right kind.

In singing in public as well as when practicing the

singer must stand so that the body will be perfectly and firmly poised. One should always stand in such a position as to be able to inhale comfortably and control a large breath, to allow the throat absolute freedom, with the head sufficiently raised to let the inflowing air penetrate all the resonance cavities.

The great thing to avoid is stiffness or discomfort of any kind in the pose. At the same time one must have a gracious air, and while feeling perfectly solidly poised on the feet, must make the impression of a certain lightness and freedom from all bodily restraint.

I have not meant in these short articles to give you anything but a very general idea of the salient points of the art of singing. After all, each one must do the real work herself.

The road is full of discouragements and hardships, but there is always something new and interesting to learn, and to achieve success, whether for the public or merely for the home circle, is worth all the trouble one can take. And so I wish you all success.

THE ART
OF SINGING

By Enrico Caruso

ENRICO CARUSO

The Career of Enrico Caruso

How a Neapolitan Mechanic's Son Became the World's Greatest Tenor

ENRICO CARUSO enjoys the reputation of being the greatest tenor since Italo Campanini. The latter was the legitimate successor of Brignoli, an artist whose wonderful singing made his uncouth stage presence a matter of little moment. Caruso's voice at its best recalls Brignoli to the veteran opera habitué. It possesses something of the dead tenor's sweetness and clarity in the upper register, but it lacks the delicacy and artistic finish of Campanini's supreme effort, although it is vastly more magnetic and thrill inspiring.

That Caruso is regarded as the foremost living tenor is made good by the fact that he is the highest priced male artist in the world. Whenever and wherever he sings multitudes flock to hear him, and no one goes away unsatisfied. He is constantly the recipient of ovations which demonstrate the power of his minstrelsy, and his lack of especial physical attractiveness is no bar to the witchery of his voice.

Caruso is a Neapolitan and is now thirty-five years of age. Unlike so many great Italian tenors, he is not of peasant parentage. His father was a skilled mechanic who had been put in charge of the warehouses of a large banking and importing concern. As a lad Enrico used to frequent the docks in the vicinity of these warehouses and became an expert swimmer at a very early age. In those halcyon days his burning ambition was to be a sailor, and he had a profound distaste for his father's plan to have him learn a trade.

At the age of ten he was still a care free and fun loving boy, without a thought beyond the docks and their life. It was then that his father ruled that since he would not become a mechanic he must be sent to school. He had already learned to read a little, but that was all. He was sent to a day school in the neighborhood, and he accepted the restraint with such bad grace that he was in almost constant disgrace. His long association with the water front had made him familiar with the art of physical defense, and he was in frequent trouble on that account.

The head master of the school was a musician, and he discovered one day that his unruly pupil could sing. He was an expert in the development of the boy soprano and he soon realized that in young Caruso he had a veritable treasure. He was shrewd enough to keep his discovery to himself for some time, for he determined to profit by the boy's extraordinary ability. The lad was rehearsed privately and was stimulated to further effort by the promise of sweetmeats and release from school duties. Finally the unscrupulous master made engagements for the young prodigy to sing at fashionable weddings and concerts, but he always pocketed the money which came from these public appearances.

At the end of the second year, when Caruso was twelve years of age, he decided that he had had enough of the school, and he made himself so disagreeable to the head master that he was sent home in disgrace. His irate father gave him a sound thrashing and declared that he must be apprenticed to a mechanical engineer. The boy took little interest in his new work, but showed some aptitude for mechanical drawing and caligraphy. In a few months he became so interested in sketching that he began to indulge in visions of becoming a great artist.

When he was fifteen his mother died, and, since he had kept at the mechanical work solely on her account, he now announced his intention of forsaking engineering and devoting himself to art and music. When his father heard of this open rebellion he fell into a great rage and declared that he would have no more of him, that he was a disgrace to the family and that he need not show his face at home.

So Caruso became a wanderer, with nothing in his absolute possession save a physique that was perfect and an optimism that was never failing. He picked up a scanty livelihood by singing at church festivals and private entertainments and in time became known widely as the most capable boy soprano in Naples. Money came more plentifully, and he was able to live generously. In a short time his voice was transformed into a marvelous alto, and he soon found himself in great demand and was surfeited with attention from the rich and powerful. It was about this time that King Edward, then Prince of Wales, heard him sing in a Neapolitan church and was so delighted that he invited the boy to go to England, an invitation which young Caruso did not accept. Now that he had "arrived" Naples was good enough for him.

One day something happened which plunged him into the deepest despair. Without a warning of any sort his beautiful alto voice disappeared, leaving in its place only the feeblest and most unmusical of croaks. He was so overcome at his loss that he shut himself up in his room and would see no one. It was the first great affliction he had ever known, and he admits that he meditated

suicide.   He had made many friends, and some of them
would have been glad to comfort him, but his grief
would admit of no partnership.

One evening when he was skulking along an obscure
highway, at the very bottom of the well of his despair,
a firm hand was laid on his shoulder and a cheery voice
called out: "Whither so fast?   Come home with me,
poor little shaver!"

It was Messiani, the famous baritone, who had always
felt an interest in the boy and who would not release
him in spite of his vigorous efforts to escape.   The big
baritone took him to his lodging and when he had suc-
ceeded in cheering the unhappy lad into a momentary
forgetfulness of his misery asked him to sing.

"But I can't," sobbed Caruso.   "It has gone!"

Messiani went to the piano and struck a chord.   The
weeping boy piped up in a tone so thin and feeble that it
was almost indistinguishable.

"Louder!" yelled the big singer, with another full
chord.   Caruso obeyed and kept on through the scale.
Then Messiani jumped up from the piano stool, seized
the astonished boy about the waist and raised him high
off his feet, at the same time yelling at the top of his
voice: "What a little jackass!   What a little idiot!"

Almost bursting with rage, for the miserable boy
thought his friend was making sport of him, Caruso
searched the apartment for some weapon with which he
might avenge himself.   Seizing a heavy brass candle-
stick, he hurled it at Messiani with all his force, but it
missed the baritone and landed in a mirror.

"Hold, madman!" interposed the startled singer.
"Your voice is not gone.   It is magnificent.   You will
be the tenor of the century."

Messiani sent him to Vergine, then the most celebrated trainer of the voice in Italy. The maestro was not so enthusiastic as Messiani, but he promised to do what he could. He offered to instruct Caruso four years, only demanding 25 per cent. of his pupil's receipts for his first five years in opera. Caruso signed such a contract willingly, although he realized afterward that he was the victim of a veritable Shylock.

When Vergine was through with the young tenor he dismissed him without lavish commendation, but with a reminder of the terms of his contract. Caruso obtained an engagement in Naples, but did not achieve marked success at once. On every payday Vergine was on hand to receive his percentage. His regularity finally attracted the attention of the manager, and he made inquiry of Caruso. The young tenor showed him his copy of the contract and was horrified to be told that he had bound himself to his Shylock for a lifetime; that the contract read that he was to give Vergine five years of actual singing. Caruso would have reached the age of fifty before the last payment came. The matter was finally adjusted by the courts, and the unscrupulous teacher lost 200,000 lire by the judgment.

In Italy every man must serve his time in the army, and Caruso was checked in his operatic career by the call to go into barracks. Not long, however, was he compelled to undergo the tedium of army life. In consideration of his art he was permitted to offer his brother as a substitute after two months, and he returned to the opera. He was engaged immediately for a season at Caserta, and from that time his rise has been steady and unimpeded. After singing in one Italian city after another he went to Egypt and thence to Paris, where he made a favorable impression. A season in Berlin followed, but the Wagner influence was dominant, and he did not succeed in restoring the supremacy of Italian opera. The next season was spent in South America, and in the new world Caruso made his first triumph. From Rio he went to London, and on his first appearance he captured his Covent Garden audience. When he made his first appearance in the United States he was already at the top of the operatic ladder, and, although many attempts to dislodge him have been made, he stands still on the topmost rung.

OF the thousands of people who visit the opera during the season few outside of the small proportion of the initiated realize how much the performance of the singer whom they see and hear on the stage is dependent on previous rehearsal, constant practice and watchfulness over the physical conditions that preserve that most precious of our assets, the voice.

Nor does this same great public in general know of what the singer often suffers in the way of nervousness or stage fright before appearing in front of the footlights, nor that his life, outwardly so fêted and brilliant, is in private more or less of a retired, ascetic one and that his social pleasures must be strictly limited.

These conditions, of course, vary greatly with the individual singer, but I will try to tell in the following articles, as exemplified in my own case, what a great responsibility a voice is when one considers that it is the great God-given treasure which brings us our fame and fortune.

I am perhaps more favored than many in the fact that my voice was always "there," and that, with proper cultivation, of course, I have not had to overstrain it in the attempt to reach vocal heights which have come to some only after severe and long-continued effort. But, on the other hand, the finer the natural voice the more sedulous the care required to preserve it in its pristine freshness to bloom. This is the singer's ever present problem—in my case, however, mostly a matter of common sense living.

As regards eating—a rather important item, by the

way—I have kept to the light "continental" breakfast, which I do not take too early; then a rather substantial luncheon toward two o'clock. My native macaroni, specially prepared by my chef, who is engaged particularly for his ability in this way, is often a feature in this midday meal. I incline toward the simpler and more nourishing food, though my tastes are broad in the matter, but lay particular stress on the excellence of the cooking, for one cannot afford to risk one's health on indifferently cooked food, no matter what its quality.

On the nights when I sing I take nothing after luncheon, except perhaps a sandwich and a glass of Chianti, until after the performance, when I have a supper of whatever I fancy within reasonable bounds. Being blessed with a good digestion, I have not been obliged to take the extraordinary precautions about what I eat that some singers do.   Still, I am careful never to indulge to excess in the pleasures of the table, for the condition of our alimentary apparatus and that of the vocal chords are very closely related, and the unhealthy state of the one immediately reacts on the other.

My reason for abstaining from food for so long before singing may be inquired. It is simply that when the large space required by the diaphragm in expanding to take in breath is partly occupied by one's dinner the result is that one cannot take as deep a breath as one would like and consequently the tone suffers and the all-important ease of breathing is interfered with.   In addition a certain amount of bodily energy is used in the process of digestion which would otherwise be entirely given to the production of the voice.

These facts, seemingly so simple, are very vital ones to a singer, particularly on an "opening night." A singer's life is such an active one, with rehearsals and performances, that not much opportunity is given for "exercise," and the time given to this must, of course, be governed by individual needs. I find a few simple physical exercises in the morning after rising, somewhat similar to those practiced in the army, or the use for a few minutes of a pair of light dumbbells, very beneficial. Otherwise I must content myself with an occasional automobile ride. One must not forget, however, that the exercise of singing, with its constant deep inhalation (and acting in itself is considerable exercise also), tends much to keep one from acquiring an oversupply of embonpoint.

A proper moderation in eating, however, as I have already said, will contribute as much to the maintenance of correct proportion in one's figure as any amount of voluntary exercise which one only goes through with on principle.

As so many of you in a number of States of this great country are feeling and expressing as well as voting opinions on the subject of whether one should or should not drink intoxicants, you may inquire what practice is most in consonance with a singer's well being, in my opinion. Here, again, of course, customs vary with the individual. In Italy we habitually drink the light wines of the country with our meals and surely are never the worse for it. I have retained my fondness for my native Chianti, which I have even made on my own Italian estate, but believe and carry out the belief that moderation is the only possible course. I am inclined to condemn the use of spirits, whisky in particular, which is so prevalent in the Anglo-Saxon countries, for it is sure to inflame the delicate little ribbons of tissue which produce the singing tone and then— *addio* to a clear and ringing high C!

Though I indulge occasionally in a cigarette, I advise all singers, particularly young singers, against this practice, which can certainly not fail to have a bad effect on the delicate lining of the throat, the vocal chords and the lungs.

You will see by all the foregoing that even the gift of a good breath is not to be abused or treated lightly, and that the "goose with the golden egg" must be most carefully nurtured.

Outside of this, however, one of the great temptations that beset any singer of considerable fame is the many social demands that crowd upon him, usually unsought and largely undesired. Many of the invitations to receptions, teas and dinners are from comparative strangers and cannot be considered, but of those from one's friends which it would be a pleasure to attend very few indeed can be accepted, for the singer's first care, even if a selfish one, must be for his health and consequently his voice, and the attraction of social intercourse must, alas, be largely foregone.

The continual effort of loud talking in a throng would be extremely bad for the sensitive musical instrument that the vocalist carries in his throat, and the various beverages offered at one of your afternoon teas it would be too difficult to refuse. So I confine myself to an occasional quiet dinner with a few friends on an off night at the opera or any evening at the play, where I can at least be silent during the progress of the acts.

In common with most of the foreign singers who come to America, I have suffered somewhat from the effects of your barbarous climate, with its sudden changes of temperature, but perhaps have become more accustomed to it in the years of my operatic work here. What has affected me most, however, is the overheating of the houses and hotels with that dry steam heat which is so trying to the throat. Even when I took a house for the season I had difficulty in keeping the air moist. Now, however, in the very modern and excellent hotel where I am quartered they have a new system of ventilation by which the air is automatically rendered pure and the heat controlled—a great blessing to the over-sensitive vocalist.

After reading the above the casual person will perhaps believe that a singer's life is really not a bit of a sinecure, even when he has attained the measure of this world's approval and applause afforded by the "great horse-shoe."

THE question, "How is it done?" as applied to the art of singing brings up so many different points that it is difficult to know where to begin or how to give the layman in any kind of limited space a concise idea of the principles controlling the production of the voice and their application to vocal art.

Every singer or singing master is popularly supposed to have a method by following out which he has come to fame. Yet if asked to describe this method many an artist would be at a loss to do so, or else deny that he had any specific method at all, such a subtle and peculiarly individual matter it is that constitutes the technical part of singing. Most singers—in fact, all of them—do many things in singing habitually, yet so inconspicuously that they could not describe how or why they did them. Yet this little set of "artistic" habits all arise from most logical causes and have become habits from their fitness to the personality of their owner and their special value in enabling that singer to do his best work by their aid. For instance, a singer will know from trials and experience just the proper position of the tongue and larynx to produce most effectively a certain note on the scale, yet he will have come by this knowledge not by theory and reasoning, but simply oft repeated attempts, and the knowledge he has come by will be valuable to him only, for somebody else would produce the same note equally well, but in quite a different way.

So one may see that there are actually as many methods as there are singers, and any particular method, even if accurately set forth, might be useless to the person who tried it. This is what I really would reply to anyone putting this question to me—that my own particular way of singing, if I have any, is, after all, peculiarly suited to me only, as I have above described.

However, there are many interesting and valuable things to be said about the voice in a general way.

Speaking first of the classification of voices, many young singers are put much in doubt and dilemma because they are unable to determine what sort of voice they really possess, whether soprano, mezzo or contralto. Of course, it is easy enough to distinguish between the extremes of these, between a "real" tenor and a low bass, but the difference between a high baritone and tenor is rather more difficult to discern, and a young man studying has often been at great disadvantage by imagining, for instance, that he had a tenor voice and trying constantly to sing music too high for him, since he in reality had only a high baritone.

In the course of development a voice very often increases its range and changes its quality sufficiently to pass from a baritone to a tenor, and it is sometimes a problem to place it during the transition process. Perhaps the surest way to determine the real character of a voice is to see on what notes words can be most easily pronounced. For the average tenor the notes up to A above middle C, for the baritone, D above middle C, and for the bass up to middle C itself, can be pronounced on the best.

One should never try to change the tessitura, or natural character of the voice. A voice will become higher just when it should by the development due to rational work and never by forcing it. Nothing is easier than to force a voice upward or downward, but to cause it to "recede," as it were, in either direction, is another matter. A baritone who tries to increase his upper range by main strength will surely in time lose his best lower notes, and a light tenor who attempts to force out notes lower than his range will never be able to sing legitimate tenor roles, and after two or three years may not be able to sing at all.

It may be well to speak now of a very important point in singing—what is called the "attack" of the tone. In general this may be described as the relative position of the throat and tongue and the quality of voice as the tone is begun. The most serious fault of many singers is that they attack the tone either from the chest or the throat. Even with robust health the finest voice cannot resist this. This is the reason one sees so many artists who have made a brilliant debut disappear from sight very soon or wind up later on a mediocre career. Singers who use their voices properly should be at the height of their talents at forty-five and keep their voices in full strength and virility up to at least fifty. At this latter age, or close after it, it would seem well to have earned the right to close one's career.

A great artist ought to have the dignity to say farewell to his public when still in full possession of his powers and never let the world apprise him of his falling off.

To have the attack true and pure one must consciously try to open the throat not only in front, but from behind, for the throat is the door through which the voice must pass, and if it is not sufficiently open it is useless to attempt to get out a full, round one; also the throat is the outlet and inlet for the breath, and if it is closed the voice will seek other channels or return quenched within.

It must not be imagined that to open the mouth wide

will do the same for the throat. If one is well versed in the art, one can open the throat perfectly without a perceptible opening of the mouth, merely by the power of respiration.

It is necessary to open the sides of the mouth, at the same time dropping the chin well, to obtain good throat opening. In taking higher notes, of course, one must open the mouth a little wider, but for the most part the position of the mouth is that assumed when smiling. It is a good idea to practice opening the throat before a mirror and try to see the palate, as when you show your throat to a doctor.

In pronouncing the sound "ah" one must always attack it in the back part of the throat, taking care, however, before uttering the syllable, to have the throat well open; otherwise what is called "stroke of the glottis" occurs and the tone formed is hard and disagreeable. If you ever hear this stroke of glottis on the attack, you may know that the singer did not attack far enough back in the throat.

The tone once launched, one must think how it may be properly sustained, and this is where the art of breathing is most concerned. The lungs, in the first place, should be thoroughly filled. A tone begun with only half filled lungs loses half its authority and is very apt to be false in pitch. To take a full breath properly, the chest must be raised at the same moment the abdomen sinks in. Then with the gradual expulsion of the breath a contrary movement takes place. The diaphragm and elastic tissue surrounding and containing the stomach and vital organs and the muscles surrounding, by practice acquire great strength and assist considerably in this process of respiration and are vital factors in the matter of controlling the supply which supports the tone. The diaphragm is really like a pair of bellows and serves exactly the same purpose. It is this ability to take in an adequate supply of breath and to retain it until required that makes or, by contrary, mars all singing. A singer with a perfect sense of pitch and all the good intentions possible will often sing off the key and bring forth a tone with no vitality to it, distressing to hear, simply for lack of breath control.

This art of respiration once acquired, the student has gone a considerable step on the road to Parnassus.

To practice deep breathing effectively it is an excellent plan to breathe through the nose, which aids in keeping the confined breath from escaping too soon. The nose also warms and filters the air, making it much more agreeable to the lungs than if taken directly through the mouth. In the practice of slow breathing make sure that the lungs are as nearly emptied as possible on the expulsion of the breath before beginning a new inspiration, as this gives extra impetus to the fresh supply of air and strengthens all the breathing muscles.

If this is not done, moreover, the effect is like two people trying to get in and out of the same narrow door at the same time.

The voice is naturally divided into three registers— the chest, medium and head. In a man's voice of lower quality this last is known as "falsetto," but in the case of a tenor he may use a tone which in sound is almost falsetto, but is really a mezza voce, or half voice. This latter legitimately belongs to a man's compass; a falsetto does not. The most important register is the medium, particularly of tenors, for this includes the greater part of the tenor's voice and can be utilized even to the top of his range if rightly produced.

In the matter of taking high notes one should remember that their purity and ease of production depend very much on the way the preceding notes leading up to them are sung. Beginning in the lower register and attacking the ascending notes well back, a balance must be maintained all the way up, so that the highest note receives the benefit and support of the original position of the throat, and there is no danger, consequently, of the throat closing and pinching the quality of the top notes.

Singers, especially tenors, are very apt to throw the head forward in producing the high notes, and consequently get that throaty, strained voice which is so disagreeable. To avoid this one should try to keep the supply of breath down as far toward the abdomen as possible, thus maintaining the upper passages to the head quite free for the emission of the voice. Remember also to sing within yourself, as it were—to feel the tones all through your being; otherwise your singing will possess no sentiment, emotion or authority. It is the failure to accomplish this which has produced so many soulless artists—singers endowed with magnificent voices, capable of surmounting every technical difficulty, but devoid of that charm of intonation which is so vital to success on the operatic stage.

I HAVE previously mentioned mezza voce and will now say a word on this subject, for the artistic use of the "half voice" is a very valuable adjunct in all singing. It may be defined simply as the natural voice produced softly, but with an extra strength of breath. It is this breathy quality, however—which one must be careful never to exaggerate or the tone will not carry—that gives that velvety effect to the tone that is so delightful.

Mezza voce is just a concentration of the full voice, and it requires, after all, as much breath support. A soft note which is taken with the "head voice" without being supported by a breath taken from the diaphragm is a helpless sort of thing. It does not carry and is inaudible at any distance, whereas the soft note which does possess the deep breath support is penetrating, concentrated and most expressive.

Another important point is that, with a "piano" note properly taken in the register which is proper to it, there is no danger of having to change the position of the throat and consequently the real character of the note when making a crescendo and again diminishing it. It will be the same note continuing to sound.

On the other hand, with a soft note taken in a register foreign to it, as soon as its strength is augmented the register must suddenly be changed and the result is like a Tyrolean yodel.

So remember in a mezza voce to see that the register is right and to use a double breath strength. I speak of the matter of register here for the benefit of those who must keep this constantly in mind. I myself have been blessed with what is called a naturally placed voice, and never had trouble with the mezza voce. The majority of Italian singers come to it easily.

There are a number of wrong sorts of voices which should be mentioned to be shunned—the "white" voice, the "throaty" voice, the "nasal" voice, and the "bleat." The nasal quality is the most difficult to correct. Many teachers, especially the French, make a point of placing the voice in the nasal cavity on the pretext of strengthening it, and this nasal quality, partly on account of the sound of many of the French words, is only too prevalent. The voice, however, can only be strengthened by legitimate means; otherwise it can easily be ruined. One can breathe through the nose, but never attack or sing through it.

The "white voice" (voce bianca) is a head voice without deep support and consequently without color; hence its appellation. One can learn to avoid it by practicing with the mouth closed and by taking care to breathe through the nose, which forces the respiration to descend to the abdomen.

The "throaty" voice comes from singing with the throat insufficiently opened, so that the breath does not pass easily through the nose and head cavities and, again, from not attacking the tone deeply enough.

To cure oneself of this throaty quality attack your notes from the abdomen, the mouth well open, standing in front of a mirror. The force of the respiration will keep the tongue depressed and the throat will remain free.

As for the fault of nasality, it is, as I have said, the most difficult to get rid of. Sometimes one never does lose it. The only remedy is what I have previously indicated—to attack from the abdomen, with the throat open, and carry the voice over the soft palate, for if the voice is placed in the nose it indicates that one is singing too far forward, which is against the rules of song. If the student has a tendency to sing in this way it is well to practice in vowel sounds only (ah-eh-ee-la-lay-lee, etc.) in order to be cured of this serious fault.

After all, however, those who have practiced the art of right breathing need have none of the defects mentioned above.

The "bleat" or goat voice, a particular fault of French singers, proceeds from the habit of forcing the voice, which, when it is of small volume, cannot stand the consequent fatigue of the larynx. Many singers with voices suitable only for light opera are constantly trying to branch out into big dramatic arias. Such performances are assuredly distressing to hear and are certainly disastrous for the voices concerned. It is no wonder that these people are often ill, for one cannot make such efforts without injuring the health. I realize that they often do it to please their directors and to be obliging in an emergency, but when they are down and out others will easily replace them and they are heard from no more.

To keep the voice fresh for the longest possible time one should not only never overstep his vocal "means," but should limit his output as he does the expenses of his purse.

There is only one way to cure a bleaty voice, and that is to cultivate an absolute rest; then, on taking up singing again, to use the "closed mouth" method until the time the strength of respiration shall be such that one can open his mouth and let the restored voice take its course.

A few words on practicing with closed mouth may here be appropriate. This method of study is really all that is necessary to place certain voices, but is bad for others. It all depends on the formation of the mouth and throat. For example, a singer troubled with the fault of closing the throat too much should never work with the mouth closed. When one can do it safely, however, it is a most excellent resource for preparatory exercises in respiration. Since, as I have already explained, breathing through the nose with closed mouth throws back the respiration to the abdomen, it is best to do the exercise seated in a comfortable, natural position.

Vocal work with closed mouth is also a powerful auxiliary to vocal agility. Many great artists perform their daily vocal exercises with the mouth shut, and I can personally testify to the excellency of this practice. It most certainly strengthens the breathing powers and at the same time rests the voice. But one should know how to do it properly. I know of many badly fatigued voices that have been restored to their normal condition in this way.

Singers, of all musicians, have the reputation of displaying the least regard for time. In operatic work, however, with an orchestra to follow or be followed, it is especially essential to observe a sane respect for the proper tempo. Otherwise one is liable to get into immediate trouble with the conductor. Of course I do not mean that one should sing in a mechanical way and give nothing of one's own personality. This would naturally rob the music of all charm. There are many singers who cannot or will not count the time properly. There are those who sing without method, who do not fit their breathing, which is really the regulator of vocal performance, to the right periods, and who consequently are never in time. They make all kinds of rallentandos where they are not necessary, to gain time to recover the breath that they have not taken when they should. It is not enough to give the notes their full value. The rests, above all, should be carefully observed in order to have sufficient opportunity to get a good breath and prepare for the next phrase. It is this exactitude that gives certainty to one's rendition and authority in singing—something many artists do not possess. A singer may make all the efforts he desires and still keep the time, and he *must* keep it.

Those who roar most loudly rarely sing in time. They give every thought to the volume of tone they are producing and do not bother themselves about anything else. The right accents in music depend very much on the exact time. Tone artists, while still making all their desired "effects" in apparent freedom of style and delivery, nevertheless do not ever lose sight of the time. Those who do are usually apt to be amateurs and are not to be imitated.

Good Diction a Requisite

GOOD diction, or the art of pronouncing the words of a song or opera properly and intelligently, is a matter sadly neglected by many singers, and indeed is not considered important by a large proportion of the audiences in this country, who do not understand foreign language, at any rate. And in an opera sung in a language unknown to most of the audience it is apparently unimportant whether the words are understood or not as long as there is a general knowledge of the plot, and the main consideration is, of course, the music.

Yet for those who are conversant with the language in which the opera is written, how common an experience it is (in concert, also) to be able, in spite of their linguistic knowledge, to understand little of what is being sung, and what a drawback this really is! How many singers there are who seem to turn all their attention to the production of beautiful sounds and neglect in most cases the words that often are equally beautiful, or should be!

One hears a great deal just now about the advisability of giving operas in the native language, as it is done in France and Germany, and the idea would seem to have its advantages, as has already been demonstrated in some excellent performances of German, French and Italian operas in English. But of what avail would such a project be if, after all, one could not understand the words of his own language as they were sung?

The language might as well be Sanskrit or Chinese.

In France the matter of diction is probably given the greatest attention, and singers at the Opera Comique, for instance, are noted for their pure and distinct enunciation of every syllable. Indeed, it is as much of a sine qua non there as good singing, if not more so, and the numerous subtleties in the French language are difficult enough to justify this special stress laid upon correct pronunciation.

It requires a very particular ability in a foreigner to attain the atmosphere of perfect French to any very high degree. Italian is generally considered an easier language to pronounce in song, as indeed it is, all the vowel sounds being full and sonorous and lacking that "covered" or mixed quality so often occurring in the French. Nevertheless, Italian has its difficulties, particularly in the way of distinctly enunciating the double consonants and proper division of the liaisons, or combining of final vowels with initial vowels, and the correct amount of softness to be given to the letter C.

All this, of course, is from the standpoint of those to whom these languages are foreign.

Certainly no singer can be called a great artist unless his diction is good, for a beautiful voice alone will not make up for other deficiencies. A singer endowed with a small voice or even one of not very pleasing quality can give more pleasure than a singer possessing a big, impressive voice, but no diction.

Some people claim that a pronunciation too distinct or too much insisted upon spoils the real voice quality, but this should not be the case if the words are correctly and naturally brought out. Doubtless, this impression has come from the fact that, particularly in France, many singers possessed of small voices must exaggerate their diction to obtain their effects. But if they did not have this perfect diction they often would have little else to recommend them. I would aver that a fine enunciation, far from interfering with it, aids the voice production, makes it softer and more concentrated, but diction should act rather as a frame for the voice and never replace it.

Each of the three languages, French, German and Italian, has its peculiar characteristics, which are of aid to the student in the general study of pronunciation, and it is well to have a knowledge of them all outside of the fact that an artist nowadays needs to have this knowledge in order not only to rank with the greatest, but to cope with the demands of an operatic career.

The Italian language in its very essence is rich in vowels and vowel combinations, from which comes principally the color in tones, and it has consequently been called the "language of song." Italians thus have naturally what it is so much trouble for singers of other nations to acquire—the numerous variations of vowel sounds.

French has the nasal sounds as its dominating characteristic and is very valuable in the cultivation of "nasal resonance."

As I said before, it is so easy to exaggerate and the voice is so apt to get too much "in the nose" that one has to be extremely careful in the use of the French "n" and "ng."

German is so full of consonants that one needs to have exceptional control of the tongue and lips to give their proper value.

English possesses the features of all the other languages—of course, in less marked degree—resembling most, perhaps, the German. The "th" is the most difficult sound to make effective in singing.

I have already spoken of the various phases of nervousness which an artist feels before the performance, but I wish to say here a word in regard to the practical significance of such nervousness. Artists who do not experience it are those who lack real genius. There are really two kinds of fear—that arising from a realization of the importance of what is to be done, the other from a lack of confidence in one's power. If a singer has no conscience in his performance he is never nervous, but full of assurance.

It is seldom that true artists are much troubled with nervousness after going upon the stage. Generally, as I have before mentioned, they are apt to be ill during the day of the performance, but before the public they forget everything and are dominated only by the real love of their art and sustained by the knowledge of possessing a proper "method."

It is certain with a good breath support even nervousness need not prevent one from singing well, although one may be actually suffering from trepidation. Yet we know that sometimes the greatest of artists are prevented thus from doing their best work. The principle, however, remains unshaken that singing in a correct way is the greatest possible "bracer."

It is best to remain absolutely quiet and see no one on the day of the performance, so as not to be enervated by the effort of talking much, to say nothing of tiring the vocal chords. One prima donna of my acquaintance occupies herself in trimming hats on the day when she sings, believing that this provides a distraction and rests her nerves. It is just as well not to "pass through" the rôle that is to be sung on the day of the appearing, but in the morning a few technical exercises to keep the voice in tune, as it were, are to be recommended. The great Italian singers of other days followed this rule, and it still holds good.

If the singer gives much of himself as well as of his voice to the public he should still hold his breathing supply in, so to speak, as he would guard the capital from which comes his income. Failure should thus be impossible if there is always a reserve to draw on. So the more one sings with good breath support the more beautiful the voice becomes. On the other hand, those who sing haphazard sometimes begin the evening well, but deteriorate more and more as the performance advances and at the end are uttering mere raucous sounds. They are like a man unable to swim who is in a deep river—their voices control them in place of they controlling their voices. They struggle vainly against obstacles, but are carried away by the flood and are finally engulfed in the waters.

Many too ambitious students are their own worst enemies in the culture of their voices. Because they have a large vocal power they want to shout all the time in spite of the repeated admonitions of their masters, who beg them to sing piano. But they hear nothing except the noise they make themselves. Such headstrong ones will never make a career, even with the finest voices in the world. Their teachers should give up trying to make them listen to reason and devote their attention to those who merit it and want to study seriously. Singing as an art is usually not considered with enough earnestness. One should go to a singing master as one goes to a specialist for a consultation and follow with the greatest care his directions. If one does not have the same respect and confidence one places in a physician it must be because the singing master does not really merit it, and it would be much better to make a change at once.

In general it is better not to stick entirely to one teacher, for it is easy to get into a rut in this way, and someone else may have a quite different and more enlightening way of setting forth his ideas.

In taking up operatic work it is understood, of course, that the singer must have mastered most of the technical difficulties, so as not to be troubled with them when they are encountered in some aria.

It is a most excellent thing to secure an engagement in one of the small theatres abroad, where one may get a large experience before trying to effect an entrance into the bigger organizations of the great capitals.

But be sure that the voice is well placed before trying any of this sort of work, and never attempt to sing a rôle above your powers in the earlier stage of your career, which otherwise may be compromised permanently.

One more bit of advice in closing. The best sort of lesson possible is to go often to the opera and note well the methods of the great artists. This personal example is worth more and is more illuminating than many precepts.

This is not so much that any form of imitation may be attempted as to teach the would-be artist how to present at his best all those telling qualities with which he may be endowed. It is the best of schools.

Pet Superstitions of Great Singers

THE most visible phase of the opera singer's life when he or she is in view of the public on the stage is naturally the one most intimately connected in the minds of the majority of people with the singer's personality, and yet there are many happenings, amusing or tragic, from the artist's point of view, which, though often seen, are as often not realized in their true significance by the audience in front of the orchestra. One might naturally think that a singer who has been appearing for years on the operatic stage in many lands would have overcome or outgrown that bane of all public performers, stage fright. Yet such is far from the case, for it seems as though the greater the artistic temperament the more truly the artist feels and the more of himself he puts into the music he sings the greater his nervousness beforehand. The latter is of course augmented if the performance is a first night and the opera has as yet been untried before a larger public.

This advance state of miserable physical tension is the portion of all great singers alike, though in somewhat varying degrees, and it is interesting to note the forms it assumes with different people. In many it is shown by excessive irritability and the disposal to pick quarrels with anyone who comes in contact with them. This is an unhappy time for the luckless "dressers," wig man and stage hands, or even fellow artists who encounter such singers before their first appearance in the evening. Trouble is the portion of all such.

In other artists the state of mind is indicated by a

stern set countenance and a ghastly pallor, while still others become slightly hysterical, laugh uproariously at nothing or burst into weeping.   I have seen a big six-foot bass singer, very popular at the opera two or three seasons ago, walking to and fro with the tears running down his cheeks for a long time before his entrance, and one of our greatest coloratura prima donnas has come to me before the opera, sung a quavering note in a voice full of emotion and said, with touching accents: "See, that is the best I can do.   How can I go on so?"

I myself have been affected often by such fright, though not always in the extreme degree above described.   This nervousness, however, frequently shows itself in one's performance in the guise of indifferent acting, singing off the key, etc.   Artists are generally blamed for such shortcomings, apparent in the early part of the production, when, as a matter of fact, they themselves are hardly conscious of them and overcome them in the course of the evening.   Yet the public, even critics, usually forget this fact and condemn an entire performance for faults which are due at the beginning to sheer nervousness.

The oft-uttered complaint that operatic singers are the most difficult to get on with of any folk, while justified, perhaps, can certainly be explained by the foregoing observations.

We of the opera are often inclined to be superstitious in a way that might annul matter of fact Americans. One woman, a distinguished and most intelligent artist, crosses herself repeatedly before taking her "cue," and a prima donna who is a favorite on two continents and who is always escorted to the theatre by her mother, invariably goes through the very solemn ceremony of kissing her mother good-by and receiving her blessing before going on to sing. The young woman feels that she could not possibly sing a note if the mother's eye were not on her every moment from the wings.

Another famous singer wears a small bracelet that was given to her when an infant by Gounod. She has grown somewhat stout of late years, and the hoop of gold has been reënforced so often that there is hardly any of the great composer's original gift left. Still, she feels that it is a charm which has made her success, and whether she sings the part of a lowly peasant or of a princess the bracelet is always visible.

And these little customs are not confined to the woman singers either, for the men are equally fond of observing some little tradition to cheer them in their performance. These little traits, trivial perhaps in themselves, are of vital importance in that they create a sense of security in the soul of the artist, who goes on his way, if not rejoicing, at least convinced that the fates are not against him.

One of the penalties paid by the singers who are much in the public eye is the constant demand made on them to listen to voices of vocal aspirants—not always very young ones, strange to say. It is sad to contemplate the number of people who think they can sing and are destined by talent and temperament for operatic careers, who have been led by misguided or foolish friends and too often by overambitious and mercenary singing masters into spending time and money on their voices in the fond hope of some day astonishing the world. Alas, they do not realize that the great singers who are heard in the New York opera houses have been picked from the world's supply after a process of most drastic selection, and that it is only the most rarely exceptional voice and talent which after long years of study and preparation become worthy to join the elect.

I am asked to hear many who have voices with promise of beauty, but who have obviously not the intelligence necessary to take up a career, for it does require considerable intelligence to succeed in opera, in spite of opinions to the contrary expressed by many. Others, who have keen and alert minds and voices of fine quality, yet lack that certain esprit and broadness of musical outlook required in a great artist. This lack is often so apparent in the person's manner or bearing that I am tempted to tell him it is no use before he utters a note. Yet it would not do to refuse a hearing to all these misfits, for there is always the chance of encountering the unknown genius, however rare a bird he may be.

And how often have the world's great voices been discovered by chance, but fortunately by some one empowered to bring out the latent gift!

One finds in America many beautiful voices, and when one thinks of the numerous singers successfully engaged in operatic careers both here and abroad, it cannot with justice be said as it used to be several years ago that America does not produce opera singers. Naturally a majority of those to whom I give a hearing here in New York are Americans, and of these are a number of really remarkable voices and a fairly good conception of what is demanded of an opera singer.

Sometimes, however, it would be amusing if it were not tragic to see how much off the track people are who have been led to think they have futures. One young man who came recently to sing for me carried a portentous roll of music and spoke in the deepest of bass voices. When asked what his main difficulty was he replied that he "didn't seem to be able to get on the key." And this was apparent when he started in and wandered up and down the tonal till he managed to strike the tonic. Then he asked me whether I would rather hear "Qui sdegno," from Mozart's "Magic Flute," or "Love Me and the World is Mine." Upon the latter being chosen he asked the accompanist to transpose it, and upon this gentleman's suggesting a third lower, he said: "No, put it down an octave." And that's where he sang it, too. I gently but firmly advised the young man to seek other paths than musical ones. However, such extreme examples as that are happily rare.

I would say to all young people who are ambitious to enter on a career of opera: Remember, it is a thoroughly hard-worked profession, after all; that even with a voice of requisite size and proper cultivation there is still a repertory of rôles to acquire, long months and years of study for this and requiring a considerable feat of memory to retain them even after they are learned. Then there is the art of acting to be studied, which is, of course, an entire occupation in itself and decidedly necessary in opera, including fencing—how to fall properly, the various gaits and gestures wherewith to portray different emotions, etc. Then, as opera is sung nowadays, the knowledge of the diction of at least three languages—French, German and Italian—if not essential, is at least most helpful.